FINDING MY STORY

Grades K-1 Inclusive After-School Program
By Mary Birdsell and Jo Meserve Mach
Photography by Mary Birdsell

FINDING MY WAY
The Finding My Way six-book series introduces kindergarten through 3rd grade children to both peers and adults with disabilities living inclusive lives.

FINDING MY STORY
The Finding My Story program challenges students to think about diversity. Using multidisciplinary activities, it also provides an opportunity for students to discover their own story.

© 2021 Mary Birdsell, Jo Meserve Mach

These activities may be reproduced solely for classroom use and may not be used or posted online.

Grades K-1: Finding My Story Inclusive After-School Program

Finding My Way Books
3512 SW Huntoon St.
Topeka, Kansas 66604
www.findingmywaybooks.com

(785) 273-6239

ISBN: 978-1-94754-133-7

Printed in the United States

10 9 8 7 6 5 4 3 2 1

For more information or to contact the author, please go to

www.findingmywaybooks.com.

Grades K - 1: Finding My Story Inclusive After-School Program

Introduction: Welcome to Finding My Way Books! Every book has several activities to use as you plan your students' participation in this program. Within each book's introduction, you will find background information about the child in the story and basic information about their disability. After reading the book and completing the activities, students write one sentence about themselves that connects them to that story. When students finish six sentences, they will have found their own story.

Co-authors: Bringing together their backgrounds in education, Occupational Therapy, and photography, Mary Birdsell and Jo Meserve Mach created Finding My Story. Mary has authored nine children's books and is a former Speech and Theatre teacher. She is also the photographer for Finding My Way Books. Jo is co-author of the Finding My Way book series and spent 36 years working as an Occupational Therapist.

BOOK	ACTIVITIES	MATERIALS
1	**I Don't Know If I Want a Puppy** (pages 1-2) **Pre-Finding My Story Survey** #1: Create a chart about animals you like #2: Visit local pet store online #3: Compare and contrast how Emma would live in different places #4: Identify shapes, draw a dog Finding My Story	✓ Survey, pencils ✓ Copies of Animals I Like ✓ Computer ✓ Copies of Emma's Home ✓ Paper and markers or sidewalk chalk ✓ Copies of Finding My Story
2	**I Want to Be Like Poppin' Joe** (pages 3-4) #1: Learn how to grow popcorn, draw popcorn growing #2: Visit Poppin' Joe's website and identify one thing you like about it #3: Investigate eating popcorn, number of bites to eat a certain amount #4: Identify jobs at your club or school, count jobs on your list Finding My Story	✓ Computer ✓ Paper and markers ✓ ¼ size paper and pencils ✓ Microwave popcorn, bowls or cups ✓ One copy of Job List ✓ Pencils ✓ Each student's Finding My Story page
3	**Kaitlyn Wants to See Ducks** (pages 5-6) #1: Learn about animals in water, roleplay #2: Visit a Sensory Inclusive Zoo online #3: use construction toys to build a zoo #4: Reader's Theater Script #5: Create a chart about Kaitlyn's family Finding My Story	✓ Computer ✓ Building toys, small animals ✓ Reader's Theater script ✓ Props needed for script ✓ Copies of Kaitlyn Family Chart ✓ Pencils ✓ Each student's Finding My Story page

Grades K - 1: Finding My Story Inclusive After-School Program

BOOK	ACTIVITIES	MATERIALS
4	**Marco and I Want to Play Ball** (pages 7-8) #1: Explore how baseball equipment feels when you're blindfolded #2: Watch a video of the book being read using sign language, learn ball, bat, and catch #3: Brainstorm how you could use slides for accessibility and fun #4: Add and subtract game Finding My Story	✓ Baseball equipment ✓ Blindfolds ✓ Computer ✓ Blocks/building toys ✓ Tokens or paper, pencils ✓ Copies of Isiah's Math Game ✓ Paper and markers ✓ Each student's Finding My Story page
5	**Waylen Wants to Jam** (pages 9-10) #1: Investigate options for drumming, collect data #2: Watch video about an animal drummer (woodpecker), research animal musicians #3: Compare and contrast drums and their pitch, draw drums #4: Count beats while drumming Finding My Story	✓ One copy of Drum Sounds ✓ Pencils ✓ Computer ✓ Paper and markers ✓ Each student's Finding My Story page
6	**OE Wants It to Be Friday** (pages 11-12) #1: Practice eight signs to use in everyday conversation #2: Watch a video on how to play boccia #3: Use construction toys to build ramps, brainstorm how they can be helpful #4: Count activities students have in common with OE Finding My Story **Finding My Story Post-Survey** **Data Collection** **Inclusive Friend Award and activity** **Amazing Reader Award**	✓ Computer ✓ Six blue balls, six red balls and one white ball or six socks of one color, six socks of another color and one white sock ✓ Blocks/building toys ✓ Copies of OE's Day, pencils ✓ Each student's Finding My Story page ✓ Copies of post-survey ✓ Paper and markers ✓ Inclusive Friend Award ✓ Amazing Reader Award

For free Teacher's Guides and literacy support visit, findingmywaybooks.com.

Grades K and 1: Finding My Story Inclusive After-School Program

Pre-Finding My Story Survey (page 13)

Directions: Have students complete surveys by circling the emoji that represents how they feel. Tell them there are no wrong answers. Collect surveys and store them for data collection. When students have completed the Inclusive After-School Program, you will compare their pre- and post-surveys.

BOOK 1: I Don't Know If I Want a Puppy

Book: Show cover of I Don't Know If I Want a Puppy.
Questions: 1. What do you think this book is about?
2. Why wouldn't someone want a puppy?
Introduction: This book is about Ethan and his older twin brothers, Joe and Jake. Ethan likes to play with cars. His brothers decide they want a puppy and keep asking Mom and Dad to get one. They have a lot to learn about caring for a puppy. Ethan watches them and learns a lot, too.
Ethan was born with a heart defect and spent a lot of time in the hospital. He had a hard time learning to speak clearly.
Understanding disabilities: Some children are born with a **heart defect**. Their heart did not form correctly before they were born, and it doesn't work right. So, they have heart surgery to fix their heart. These babies need extra care because they can get sick easily. Their development or learning is often delayed.
Read aloud: I Don't Know If I Want a Puppy and show photos on each page

Activity #1

Question: What animal do you think is the most popular pet?
Activity: Hand out pencils and Animals I Like (page 14). Students are to rank 1-4 how much they like each animal, with #1 being their favorite. Students need to write a sentence describing what they like about this animal. For example, I like to walk a dog. Taking turns, have students share their charts and what they like about their #1 ranked animal.

Rank	Animal	What I like about this animal
	Dog	
	Cat	
	Fish	
	Bird	

Activity #2

Question: Where can you buy a pet? (pet store, friend, animal shelter)

Activity: Have students look at your local pet store online or plan a visit to the store. Also, you could visit an animal shelter. Ask students to talk about the most interesting animal they see.

Activity #3

Introduction: Emma lives with Ethan and his family in a house. Emma plays in their yard and Ethan takes her for neighborhood walks.

Question: Where else do dogs live with people?

Activity: This activity helps students compare and contrast how Emma would live in different environments. Pass out pencils and Emma's Home (page 15). Together, answer these questions:
1. Where does Emma go in her house?
2. Where would Emma go if she lived on a farm?
3. Where would Emma go if she lived in an apartment?

	Emma's Activities
House	plays in backyard, neighborhood walks, sleeps in dog house
Farm	runs outside, plays outside, sleeps outside
Apartment	walks in the park, plays inside, sleeps inside

Activity #4

Book: Show pages 12 and 23 from I Don't Know If I Want a Puppy. Ask students to look at Emma's shape.

Activity: On the board draw a rectangle, circle, triangle, and square. Ask students to name the shapes as you point to each one. Give students paper and markers and ask them to draw a picture of Emma using those shapes. Or go outside and have students draw with sidewalk chalk. Taking turns, have students share their drawings with the group. (*Emma could have a circle for her face, rectangle for her body, thin rectangles for legs and tail, triangles for ears.*)

Finding My Story

Introduction: Ethan likes to play with cars. He isn't sure about their family having a puppy.

Question: When have you been unsure of doing something new?

Activity: Pass out pencils and copies of the Finding My Story activity (page 16). Have students fill in sentence #1 with something they are unsure about doing and what they might learn. For example, I don't know if I want to work in a garden, but I might learn to grow something to eat. Taking turns, student share their sentence. Collect papers and store them where it is convenient to get them when you need to pass them back to the students to continue working on sentences for their stories.

BOOK 2: I Want to Be Like Poppin' Joe

Book: Show cover of I Want to Be Like Poppin' Joe.
Questions: 1. What do you think this book is about?
    2. Why would someone want to be like Poppin' Joe?
Introduction: Poppin' Joe is an adult with Down syndrome and autism. When he was growing up, he liked to vacuum, take swimming lessons, and play with his older siblings. Today, Joe has his own business and lives in his own apartment with a support worker.

Dylan is a kindergartner with Down syndrome. Dylan loves to be with his older brother, play with his dog, and be outside. He likes to help his dad in the yard and cook with his mom.

Understanding disabilities: Children with **Down syndrome** have difficulty learning new things. Some are slower learning to walk or slower learning to talk. They are slower thinkers, which means they need more time to learn. Children born with **autism** think and feel differently. This makes it hard for them to communicate because they don't understand how others think and feel.

Read aloud: I Want to Be Like Poppin' Joe and show photos on each page.

Activity #1
Discussion: Where does popcorn come from?
Activity: Look at https://www.wikihow.com/Grow-Popcorn and talk about the pictures showing how to grow popcorn. Pass out paper and markers and have students draw their own pictures of how to grow popcorn.

Activity #2
Introduction: Poppin' Joe has a business and a website.
Activity: Go to Findingmywaybooks.com and click on Interviews with Kids on the menu. Find Dylan's picture and click. Scroll down Dylan's page. At the bottom is the link to Poppin' Joe's Gourmet Popcorn website. Have students scroll through Poppin' Joe's website and each share one thing they like about the website.

Activity #3
Introduction: We're going to investigate eating popcorn.
Question: How many bites of popcorn will it take to eat a bowl of popcorn?
Activity: Pass out ¼ size pieces of paper, pencils and small bowls of popcorn. Each student needs to eat their popcorn slowly so they can mark their paper every time they take a bite. When their bowls are empty, have students total the number of marks. Ask students to report their total. Write each student's name on the board and their number of bites. Ask students to identify who took the most bites and who took the fewest bites.

Activity #4

Introduction: There are many jobs being done at your club or in your community.

Activity: As a group, brainstorm the jobs at your club or school. You can help students think of staff names and then figure out their jobs. Use the Job List (page 17) to record the jobs and then to count them.

Finding My Story

Introduction: Dylan wants to be like Poppin' Joe. He likes Joe, and he likes what he does.

Activity: Students need to think about someone they admire. Hand out Finding My Story pages. Have students fill in sentence #4 with a person's name they admire and why they admire this person. For example, I want to be like Raven because she is nice to everyone. Students take turns reading their sentence to the group. Collect papers.

BOOK 3: Kaitlyn Wants to See Ducks

Book: Show cover of Kaitlyn Wants to See Ducks.

Questions: 1. What do you think this book is about?

2. Why do you think Kaitlyn wants to see ducks?

Introduction: Kaitlyn is a 1st grader with Down syndrome. She and her younger twin sisters love to visit the zoo. Kaitlyn also likes to play in water. Their family has a rubber swimming pool in their backyard that they all like to play in together.

Understanding disabilities: Children with **Down syndrome** have difficulty learning new things. Some are slower learning to walk or slower learning to talk. They are slower thinkers, which means they need more time to learn.

Read aloud: Kaitlyn Wants to See Ducks and show photos on each page.

Activity #1

Introduction: All animals use water. For example, dolphins jump in water.

Question: How do the animals in Kaitlyn's story use water? (apes play in it, giraffes drink it, elephants take a bath in it, ducks swim in it)

Activity: Create a list of the student responses to the question. Have students stand in a circle and imagine they are in water. Together, have them make the actions and pretend to play, drink, bathe, and then swim. Have students brainstorm why all these actions are important to animals.

Activity #2

Introduction: Kaitlyn loves to see ducks at her community zoo. Every zoo is different. It's fun to visit different zoos.

Activity: Go to Findingmywaybooks.com and click on Interviews with Kids on the menu. Find Kaitlyn's picture and click. Scroll down Kaitlyn's page. At the bottom is the link to a Sensory Inclusive Zoo website. Ask students to identify what is different about this zoo.

Activity #3

Introduction: In Kaitlyn's book, you visit a zoo. You see where many animals live.

Question: What do you remember about the zoo Kaitlyn and her family visited?

Activity: Explain to students they are going to build a zoo and decide where they want their animals to live. Provide building blocks and small animals to small groups and have them build their own zoo. When finished, have everyone walk around the room and visit all the zoos!

Activity #4
Reader's Theater Script for Kaitlyn Wants to See Ducks. (pages 18-20)

Activity #5
Introduction: Mom, Dad, Paige, Alexis and Kaitlyn like different animals in the zoo. To compare their favorite animals, we're going to each create a chart and see which animal each family member likes.
Activity: Pass out Kaitlyn's Family Chart (page 20) and pencils. Have students place an X in the box that matches the animals each family member likes. Next, have students place an X in the boxes that match the animals they like. Finally, have students add each column to get the number of animals each person likes.

	Kaitlyn	Mom	Dad	Paige	Alexis	Me
Apes			X	X	X	
Lions			X			
Elephants			X			
Giraffes			X	X	X	
Goats		X	X	X	X	
Bears			X	X	X	
Ducks	X		X			
Total number	1	1	7	4	4	

Finding My Story
Introduction: Kaitlyn wants to see ducks. We all have animals we like.

Activity: This activity has students think about an animal they want to see and why they like it. Pass out pencils and Finding My Story activity pages. Have students fill in sentence #2 with an animal they want to see and why. For example, I want to see snakes because they are good at hiding. Taking turns, have student share what they have written. Collect papers.

BOOK 4: Marco and I Want to Play Ball

Book: Show cover of Marco and I Want to Play Ball.
Questions: 1. What do you think this book is about?
2. What kind of ball game do you think they want to play?
Introduction: Marco and Isiah are cousins and best friends. Isiah is in 1st grade and Marco will start kindergarten soon. They love to spend time in the country with their grandparents and play ball with Grandpa.

Isiah has Spina bifida. It was difficult for him to learn to walk. Since his favorite thing to do has always been to play with balls, he plays different games with balls to get stronger. Isiah wears leg braces to help his legs stay in the correct position. He isn't able to run, but his cousin Marco doesn't care. He just wants to play with Isiah.

Understanding disabilities: When children have **Spina bifida,** their spinal cord or the nerves in their spine have not developed correctly. Some use a wheelchair and others use leg braces to help them move. Otherwise, they can do everything that all children can do.

Read aloud: Marco and I Want to Play Ball and show photos on each page.

Activity #1
Introduction: Marco and Isiah play baseball with Grandpa. They use a white ball with red stitches.
Questions: 1. What other games use a ball?
2. How are balls different for each game?
Activity: This activity teaches how to identify equipment used in baseball by its feel rather than by looking at its shape and color. Give each student a blindfold and a piece of equipment. Taking turns, students describe their item in as much detail as possible. (shape, smell, texture, weight)

Activity #2
Introduction: Often we read books out loud. If someone who is deaf wants to hear the story, they aren't able to hear it.
Question: How could you read a book to someone who is deaf? (use sign language)
Activity: Go to Findingmywaybooks.com and click on Interviews with Kids on the menu. Click on Isiah, scroll down the page, and find the video of a girl signing Marco and I Want to Play Ball. As you watch the video, ask students to pay attention so they can learn the signs for ball, bat, and catch. After the video, have students stand and practice the three signs they've learned

Activity #3

Book: Show page 10 in Marco and I Want to Play Ball.
Questions: 1. Why does Isiah use a slide?
2. Does Marco need to use a slide?
Discussion: Isiah has leg braces to help him walk, it's too hard for him to run. He uses a slide to save time. It helps him feel included because Marco and Grandpa don't have to wait while he walks the long distance to get ready to bat.
Activity: Have students brainstorm activities to do with a slide. Encourage them to consider ways to use a slide in different places in their club or school. After brainstorming, have students draw a picture of their ideas to share with the club director or school principal.

Activity #4

Book: Show page 11 of Marco and I Want to Play Ball.
Question: Why do Marco and Isiah need to pick up balls?
Activity: Divide group into pairs. Pass out 20 tokens (or paper to tear into small pieces and crush into 20 small balls) to each pair. Pass out Isiah's Math Game (page 22) and pencils. Have students count the number of balls in the photo and set out seven tokens. Read out loud the following three math problems. Together the pairs solve the problem using their tokens and then filling out their game page. Taking turns, have each pair share the problem they created.

1. Add 2, subtract 3, add 10 = 16
2. Subtract 4, add 9, subtract 8 = 4
3. Add 3, subtract 5, add 4 = 9
4. Pairs create their own problem.

$$7 + 2 = 9 - 3 = 6 + 10 = 16$$
$$7 - 4 = 3 + 9 = 12 - 8 = 4$$
$$7 + 3 = 10 - 5 = 5 + 4 = 9$$

Finding My Story

Introduction: Marco wants to play with Isiah and they both want to play ball with Grandpa.
Question: Do you have a favorite person? What do you like to do together?
Activity: Pass out pencils and each student's Finding My Story page. Have students fill in sentence #3 with someone's name and what they want to do together. For example, Maria and I want to twirl. Taking turns, have student share what they have written. Collect papers.

BOOK 5: Waylen Wants to Jam

Book: Show the cover of Waylen Wants to Jam.

Question: 1. What do you think this book is about?
   2. Who do you think Waylen jams with?

Introduction: Waylen is a 3rd grader. He has always loved to drum. When he was little, he banged on everything to make noise. His older brother started playing the drums, and he wanted to learn to play the drums, too.

Waylen was born with autism. He is the first autistic child on his community drumline.

Understanding disabilities: Children born with **autism** think and feel differently than other children. This makes it hard for them to communicate. They don't understand how others think and feel. They can learn differently, and they also have their own interests.

Read: Read aloud Waylen Wants to Jam.

Activity #1

Introduction: There are many kinds of drums. Waylen plays a snare drum and a bass drum. You can also make drumming sounds with everyday objects.

Question: What do you need to make a drumming sound? Do you need drumsticks?

Activity: We're going to investigate drums in this room. Have students find something to be their drum. Hand out pencils and have one copy of Drum Sounds (page 23) to pass around. Taking turns, students show off their drumming ability. Have students fill out a line on the chart with their name, what they use as a drum and how it sounds.

Name	Drum	How my drum sounds

Activity #2

Introduction: Waylen likes to play the drums. He loves to make music. Animals like to make music, too.

Question: Which animal makes sounds like a drummer? (woodpecker)

Activity: Visit https://www.youtube.com/watch?v=ewfTDsKKCWA to watch the video of a woodpecker drumming. Have students research online other animals that make music and have them share what they discover. Examples: whales hum, birds sing, elephants trumpet.

Activity #3

Introduction: Different drums make distinct sounds. This means they each have their own pitch. It is a low pitch when the top of the drum is large. When the top of the drum is small, it makes a high pitch.

Question: What is the difference between the pitch of a snare drum (page 2) and a bass drum (page 23)?

Activity: Pass out paper and markers. Have students design a drum with a high pitch and a drum with a low pitch. Taking turns, students share their pictures with the group.

Activity #4

Introduction: Waylen shares he drums by counting 1-2-3-4-5-6-7-8. When you play the drum, you need to count the beats.

Activity: Each student finds a place to drum. Practice counting the beats and drumming together. Sing a song as you drum or count out loud together: one and two and three and four, repeating the phrase and hitting the drum with each number.

Finding My Story

Introduction: Waylen wants to jam. He wants to be a drummer!

Question: What do you want to do?

Activity: Pass out pencils and each student's Finding My Story page. Students need to fill in sentence #5 with sometime they'd like to learn to do. For example, I want to learn to fly a kite. Taking turns, students share their sentences. Collect papers.

BOOK 6: OE Wants It to Be Friday

Book: Show the cover of OE Wants It to Be Friday.
Questions: 1. What do you think this book is about?
2. What do you think happens on Friday?
Introduction: OE spent the first five years of her life in Russia living in a crib. When her US parents adopted her, they wanted her to learn to do as much as she could for herself. They got her equipment to help: a wheelchair, standing straps, and a communication board. She is seven years old and goes to school.
Understanding disabilities: OE and her coach Austin were born with **cerebral palsy**. Cerebral means the brain. Palsy means there's a problem with how you move. OE's and Austin's brains don't send the correct messages to their muscles, so they can't move their body very well or use their voice to talk. Both OE and Austin are very smart in doing schoolwork. They are very good at learning and they also have their own interests.
Read aloud: OE Wants It to Be Friday and show photos on each page.

Activity #1

Introduction: OE isn't able to talk. She uses communication devices or sign language. Sign language is fun to learn!
Activity: Below are eight basic signs. Have students stand in a circle and practice the signs.

Activity #2

Introduction: Austin and OE play boccia. Austin is a United States Boccia player and has won many championships. It would be fun to learn how to play boccia.
Activity: Have your group watch https://www.youtube.com/watch?v=78XSl99ftc4 to learn how to play boccia. It shows how to play with rolled up socks instead of balls. Using balls or socks, have students practice playing boccia.

Activity #3

Questions: 1. Where do you see ramps in OE's book? (pages 4, 15, and 19.)
          2. Why does OE use ramps?
Activity: Using blocks and other building toys, see how many ramps your students can make. Have students explain how their ramps could be helpful to someone.

Activity #4

Question: What does OE do in her story?
Activity: Hand out OE's Day (page 24) and pencils. Follow the directions on activity sheet to have students count how many activities OE does each week, how many activities they have in common with OE, and how many times they do each activity a week.
Question: How many activities do you have in common with OE?
Activity: Ask students to hold the numbers of fingers up that match the number of activities they have in common with OE.

Finding My Story

Introduction: OE wants it to be Friday. That's her favorite day of the week because she loves to learn to play boccia with Austin.
Question: Do you have a favorite day?
Activity: Pass out pencils and each student's Finding My Story page. Have students fill in sentence #6 with their favorite day and what they enjoy doing. For example, I want it to be Monday so I can have lunch with Grandma. They have now found their story and all their sentences are complete. Taking turns, have students read their stories.

Post-Finding My Story Survey (page 25)

Directions: Have students complete surveys by circling the emoji that represents how they feel. Tell them there are no wrong answers. Collect the surveys.
Now that students have completed the Inclusive Afterschool Program, you can use the Data Collection form to compare their pre- and post-surveys.

Data Collection (page 26)

This form helps you summarize, compare, and analyze pre- and post-survey results.

Inclusive Friend Award (page 27)

Activity: Hand out paper and markers. Have students draw a picture of themselves being inclusive. Encourage students to share ideas they have learned about being an inclusive friend in their club, school, and community. Pass out Inclusive Friend Awards to all students.

Amazing Reader Award (page 28) for students who read all six books.

Pre-Finding My Story Survey

Name _____   Date_____

Circle the emoji that best fits you.

	Don't know what to do!	Get nervous. Do nothing.	Smile	Talk
What do I do when I meet someone in a wheelchair?	😳	😐	🙂	😃
What do I do when I meet someone who looks different because of a disability?	😳	😐	🙂	😃
What do I do when I want to play with someone with a disability?	😳	😐	🙂	😃
What do I do when I want to talk to someone I know with a disability?	😳	😐	🙂	😃
How do I feel about being an inclusive friend?	😳	😐	🙂	😃

Name _____

Animals I Like

Directions: Rank the animals 1-4 with #1 as the animal you like the most. Write a sentence about what you like about each animal.

Rank	Animal	What I like about this animal
	Dog	_____
	Cat	_____
	Fish	_____
	Bird	_____

Name _____

Emma's Home

Directions: Think about what Emma would do if she lived in different places.
Answer each question by filling in the box under Emma's activities.

1. Where does Emma go when she's at her house?
2. Where would Emma go if she lived on a farm?
3. Where would Emma go if she lived in an apartment?

	Emma's activities
House	
Farm	
Apartment	

Finding My Story

My name is _____

Directions: After you read each book and complete the activities, you're ready to work on finding your story. Fill in the blanks for the sentence connected to the book you've just finished reading.

1. I don't know if I want to _____,

    but I might learn to_____.

2. I want to be like _____ because

    _____.

3. I want to see_____ because

    _____.

4. _____ and I want to_____.

5. I want to _____.

6. I want it to be _____ so I can_____

    _____.

Job List

Directions: Make a list of different jobs in your building. Count how the number of jobs.

_____   _____

_____   _____

_____   _____

_____   _____

_____   _____

_____   _____

_____   _____

_____   _____

_____   _____

_____   _____

How many jobs are on your list? _____

Kaitlyn Wants to See Ducks: Reader's Theater Script

Roles: Narrator, Kaitlyn, Mom, Dad, Alexis, Paige, apes (mom and baby), lions (1 or 2), giraffes (2), goats (mom and baby), bears (2), ducks (5-10)

Props: toys for apes to play with, pretend dirt, pretend green leaves to feed giraffes

Setting: a zoo

NARRATOR: It's family day at the zoo.

    This is Kaitlyn.

    She loves to swim.

    Ducks love to swim, too.

    Kaitlyn thinks ducks are the best animals.

KAITLYN: Let's see ducks!

MOM: I think there are a lot of fun animals.

    Let's go see the apes.

KAITLYN: Let's see ducks.

DAD: Kaitlyn, are the apes outside or inside?

NARRATOR: They are inside. (*Mom and baby ape play.*)

ALEXIS and PAIGE: We like the baby ape.

NARRATOR: Kaitlyn likes the water falling.

    It's loud and wet.

    Those apes are silly.

    Those silly apes don't swim.

KAITLYN: Let's see ducks.

MOM: (Mom *roars like a lion and does sign language for lion.*)

    Who lives next door?

ALEXIS and PAIGE: (*Alexis and Paige do sign language for lion.*)

    The lions, the lions!

Kaitlyn Wants to See Ducks: Reader's Theater Script

DAD: Stand close. (*The lions are sleeping.*)

    Can you hear the lions?

NARRATOR: No, the lions are sleeping.

    Those sleepy lions don't swim.

KAITLYN: Let's see ducks. (*Kaitlyn is lying on the ground.*)

MOM: Who can sign elephant? (*Mom signs elephant.*)

NARRATOR: Will the elephants get a bath? (*The elephants play in the dirt.*)

    No, not today.

    They play in the dirt.

    Those dirty elephants don't swim.

KAITLYN: Let's see ducks! (*Kaitlyn is yelling.*)

MOM: Who wants to feed the giraffes?

ALEXIS and PAIGE: We want to feed the giraffes. (*They feed giraffes some leaves.*)

NARRATOR: Those hungry giraffes don't swim.

KAITLYN: Let's see ducks.

DAD: The goats and bears are next.

NARRATOR: Kaitlyn looks at her family.

    Mom likes to talk to animals. (*Mom talks to the goats.*)

    Alexis likes to feed the animals.

    Paige likes to find baby animals.

    Dad likes to see all the animals. (*Dad watches the bears play.*)

KAITLYN: Let's see ducks. (*Kaitlyn holds her head and is upset.*)

DAD: It's time to see ducks!

Kaitlyn Wants to See Ducks: Reader's Theater Script

NARRATOR: Oh no, where are the ducks? (*The ducks are hiding.*)

    Dad looks for ducks.

    Mom looks for ducks.

    Alexis looks for ducks.

    Paige looks for ducks.

    Kaitlyn looks for ducks.

NARRATOR: Kaitlyn's family wants to help her find the ducks.
    (*The ducks come out of their hiding places.*)

    Kaitlyn sees something silly.   (*One duck has its bottom in the air.*)

    Kaitlyn sees ducks sleeping.

    Kaitlyn sees dirty ducks.

    Kaitlyn sees hungry ducks.

    Kaitlyn sees ducks swimming.

    Kaitlyn is happy.

    She found her ducks.

Name _____

 # Kaitlyn's Family Chart

Directions: Fill in the chart below.
Make an X in the boxes that show the animals each person likes.
Count the number of Xs each person has in their column.

	Kaitlyn	Mom	Dad	Paige	Alexis	Me
Apes						
Lions						
Elephants						
Giraffes						
Goats						
Bears						
Ducks						
Total						

Name _____

 ## Isiah's Math Game

Directions: Listen to your teacher read out loud the first three problems.
 Fill in the blanks.
 Then make up your own problem.

7 + ____ = ____ − ____ = ____ + ____ = ____

7 − ____ = ____ + ____ = ____ − ____ = ____

7 + ____ = ____ − ____ = ____ + ____ = ____

7 □ ____ = ____ □ ____ = ____ □ ____ = ____

Drum Sounds

Directions: Each student writes their name, what they are using for a drum, and how their drum sounds.

Name	Drum	How my drum sounds

Name _____

OE's Day

Directions: Mark with an X the activities that you do from OE's list.
Fill in how many times a week you do each activity.
Add the activities you have in common with OE
Add the number of times you do your activities.

OE's Weekly Activities	I also do these activities.	Number of times I do this activity in a week.
Choose clothes to wear to school		
Go to the store with Mom		
Sing with the car radio		
Study for a spelling test		
Play a game with my family		
Dance		
Play boccia		
TOTAL		

Post-Finding My Story Survey

Name _____   Date _____

Circle the emoji that best fits you.

	Don't know what to do!	Get nervous. Do nothing.	Smile	Talk
What do I do when I meet someone in a wheelchair?	😳	😐	🙂	😃
What do I do when I meet someone who looks different because of a disability?	😳	😐	🙂	😃
What do I do when I want to play with someone with a disability?	😳	😐	🙂	😃
What do I do when I want to talk to someone I know with a disability?	😳	😐	🙂	😃
How do I feel about being an inclusive friend?	😳	😐	🙂	😃

Data Collection for Finding My Story

Organization: _____ Prepared by: _____

Number of participants: _____ Pre-survey date: _____ Post-survey date: _____

Description: Each survey contains the following questions with responses selected from an Emoji Likert type scale.

1. What do I do when I meet someone in a wheelchair?
2. What do I do when I meet someone who looks different because of a disability?
3. What do I do when I want to play with someone with a disability?
4. What do I do when I want to talk to someone I know with a disability?
5. How do I feel about being an inclusive friend?

Scoring: Each Emoji has an assigned value. Total the number of responses for each Emoji.

Don't know what to do! = 1
Get nervous. Do nothing = 2
Smile = 3
Talk = 4

Multiply the number of participants X 5 questions to identify the total number of responses. _____ Divide the number of responses per Emoji by the total to get percentage scores.

Pre-survey:

- _____% of the responses were *'Don't know what to do!'*
- _____% of the responses were *'Get nervous. Do nothing.'*
- _____% of the responses were *'Smile'*
- _____% of the responses were *'Talk'*

Post-survey:

- _____% of the responses were *'Don't know what to do!'*
- _____% of the responses were *'Get nervous. Do nothing.'*
- _____% of the responses were *'Smile'*
- _____% of the responses were *'Talk'*

Summary: Compare the pre-and post-survey results to provide a general overview of change in participants attitudes. For additional information, you could score each question to identify where attitude changes occurred. Also, consider including anecdotal data and staff observations during the program.

Finding My Story Certificate

Inclusive After-School Program

Inclusive Friend Award

For building an inclusive community one friend at a time!

Awarded to

_____

_____

Signature and Date

Finding My Story

Amazing Reader Award

I Don't Know If I Want a Puppy

I Want to Be Like Poppin' Joe

Kaitlyn Wants to See Ducks

Marco and I Want to Play Ball

Waylen Wants to Jam

OE Wants It to Be Friday

For doing an amazing job reading six Finding My Way books!

Awarded to

_____

_____

Signature and Date

www.ingramcontent.com/pod-product-compliance
Lightning Source LLC
Chambersburg PA
CBHW051403110526
44592CB00023B/2935